Hawaiian Spirulina®
Superfood for Super Health

By Gerald Cysewski, Ph.D.

Publisher's Note

Disclaimer. The information in this book is for educational purposes only; it is not intended to be taken as medical advice or as an attempt to sell a particular product, nor is it intended to diagnose, treat, cure, or prevent any disease. The opinions expressed are those of the author. People with medical problems or questions should consult a health professional. **Animal Research is never conducted by the publisher.** Animal Research Policy: Cyanotech Corporation, the publisher of this book, does not condone animal experimentation. As a service to the reader, animal studies conducted by others are reported in this book so readers may fully understand the ongoing medical research and the potential benefits of spirulina in human nutrition.

Reproduction of Contents. This book may not be reproduced in whole or in part, by any means, without written permission from Cyanotech Corporation, 73-4460 Queen Kaahumanu Highway, Suite 102, Kailua-Kona, HI 96740 USA or email info@cyanotech.com.

Table of Contents

Introduction
By William Sears, M.D.

Nearly 20 years ago, after suffering a life-threatening illness and needing to transform my health, I discovered that some of the healthiest superfoods come from the sea. So, I went "fishing" for these superfoods.

My first "catch" was omega-3 fats found in oily fish, especially wild Pacific salmon. This discovery led to my first book about that nutrient: *The Omega-3 Effect*, published in 2012.

The next healthy catch came while fishing in Alaska with Randy Hartnell, former Alaskan fisherman and owner of an online provider of sustainable seafood. One day while watching a salmon run, I asked Randy, "Why are wild salmon so pink?"

The answer led to my next book: *Natural Astaxanthin: Hawaii's Supernutrient* published in 2015. The pink color that you see in salmon comes from a nutrient called astaxanthin that is present in the marine food chain. Microalgae produce astaxanthin to withstand the intense conditions they're subjected to in the marine environment. It's one of the most protective substances in the world, which is why it's so healthful for us to ingest in our bodies.

In my never-ending quest for seafood superfoods, I decided to visit a farm in Hawaii where astaxanthin is grown commercially, and that's where I discovered spirulina. Spirulina is another species of microalgae, the super seaplant that has many very attractive health benefits. I've always advocated getting your nutrients from healthy food, not supplement pills. But I realize that many people don't get the nutrients they need from food, so supplements solve a problem in many people's diets. For example, if you're not eating three to four servings of wild salmon each week, you're probably not getting enough omega-3s or astaxanthin, and should consider supplementing your diet with them each day.

But that's one of the beautiful things about spirulina—it's not a supplement. Spirulina is a super-healthy food. In fact, spirulina has been referred to as a "superfood" for many years because it's so packed with nutrients that just one teaspoon of the leading brand, Hawaiian Spirulina, delivers a variety of vitamins, minerals, calcium, iron, and protein. Hawaiian Spirulina is especially high in antioxidants, which are nutrients that support longevity and a healthy immune system. And as a "show-me-the-science" doctor, I was extremely pleased to find out that there are hundreds of medical research studies showing a wide range of health benefits from Hawaiian Spirulina—from supporting cardiovascular health to simply boosting people's everyday energy levels.

I've been back to the microalgae farm in Hawaii multiple times since my original visit there a few years ago. I've had the pleasure of meeting the founder of the spirulina farm, Dr. Gerry Cysewski. I am extremely impressed with the quality his company puts into its products and its focus on research. Hawaiian Spirulina grows on the only farm in the world that adds deep seawater to its spirulina ponds. The water comes from 2,000 feet below the surface of the Pacific Ocean, and so it hasn't been exposed to the surface for thousands of years. It's the purest water you can find anywhere, full of rich minerals. Dr. Cysewski and his staff really care about health and the quality of the product that bears the Hawaiian Spirulina name.

In just a few years, I've gone from spirulina novice to spirulina enthusiast. In fact, I'm so enthusiastic about Hawaiian Spirulina that not only do I add it to my smoothies each morning, but I've also written a book about spirulina for children, called *My Big Green Smoothie*. Spirulina's not just good for adults like me, it's a wonderful food for people of all ages who need to eat what Dr. Mother Nature prescribes: superfood for super health.

Chapter

1

Spirulina: The Blue-Green Superfood

What Is Spirulina?

Spirulina is a "superfood." It is the most nutritious, concentrated whole food known to humankind. It has a rich, vibrant history, and occupies an intriguing biological and ecological niche in the plant kingdom. Spirulina is a spiral-shaped, blue-green microalgae that grows naturally in the wild in freshwater lakes, natural springs, and saltwater. Its deep blue-green color is what gives the water its greenish hue. Spirulina is also cultivated and harvested in man-made reservoirs around the world.

For centuries, civilizations the world over have cultivated and cherished spirulina for its health-improving benefits. The Aztecs harvested the microalgae from Lake Texcoco in Mexico. The native people in Chad, Africa, have used the microalgae as a staple of their daily diet because of its concentrated nutritional value and prolific growth in the pure saltwater lakes of the region.

Spirulina is made of between 55 and 70 percent protein (more than beef, chicken, and soybeans), all the essential and non-essential amino acids, as well as high levels of iron; beta carotene; minerals and multivitamins, including vitamin B12; and phycocyanin, a pigment-protein antioxidant complex found only in blue-green microalgae. These nutrients are lacking in most diets.

Spirulina provides people with long-lasting energy and strengthens the immune system. Its antioxidant power contributes to the entire body operating in optimal condition; it enables children and others who don't like vegetables to still "eat their greens;" and it helps busy people who don't have time for regular, balanced meals to maintain their nutrition.

Where Does Spirulina Come From?

Microalgae were the first life form to appear on the planet. Billions of years ago, they transformed the carbon-dioxide-based atmosphere to an oxygen-rich atmosphere in which other life forms could evolve.

Most people are familiar with the large green or red algae growing in lakes and the ocean. These are commonly known as seaweed. By contrast, microalgae are tiny, one-celled organisms that come in different species depending on their phytopigment and phytonutrient content. These microalgae are extensively researched for their health-giving benefits.

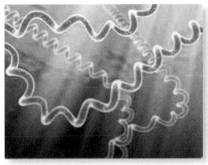

Spirulina cells

Of the more than 30,000 species of microalgae, blue-green microalgae, such as spirulina, are the most primitive. They contain no nucleus and their cell walls are soft and easily digested, unlike those of other plants that contain hard cellulose walls. Of all the microalgae, spirulina has emerged as the most potent and nutritious.

Commercial production of spirulina began over 45 years ago from a single lake on the outskirts of Mexico City. The Mexican company skimmed the spirulina from the surface of the lake, air-dried it, then sold it to supplement brands, primarily in the United States and Europe. Unfortunately, the lake suffered from being too close to Mexico City, and the spirulina soaked up all the heavy metals and lead in the air and water from the nearby polluted metropolis, destroying spirulina's most fragile and health-giving nutrients.

To fill the void in the marketplace for safe and nutritious spirulina, the microalgae company Cyanotech began an exhaustive search lasting two years to find the ideal conditions in which to cultivate high-quality spirulina. The Kona coast of Hawaii's pristine Big Island was selected for its size, low population density, pure water access, state protection and temperate climate.

The Big Island, as Hawaii Island has come to be known, has the largest area of all the Hawaiian Islands, but also one of the lowest population densities. There is no agricultural runoff of fertilizers or pesticides, nor are there golf courses in the area that could affect the quality of the ponds. Furthermore, the Big Island has an almost constant on-shore breeze that knocks back any potential manmade air pollution.

Not only does the Kona coast have clean air, it also has pure water. Cyanotech's water supply begins with rainwater that gets naturally filtered through lava rock. It is this pure drinking water that fills the ponds in which spirulina grows.

The Kona coast has also been designated as a BioSecure zone, which prohibits any genetically modified organisms or other unnatural substances. This ensures that the 90-acre Hawaiian Spirulina farm is a pure and natural environment for growing microalgae.

Spirulina needs mild temperatures and plenty of sunshine. Kona is the sunniest coastal location in the United States, making it the only spirulina farm in the world that is able to grow spirulina year-round.

Who Should Take Spirulina?

People of All Ages

Now that people are living longer, the desire to stay strong and healthy is as ardent as ever. But because most people lead such busy lives, meals end up being quickly prepared and quickly consumed.  People want their food to be healthy, but they also want it now. The Centers for Disease Control and Prevention recommends that five to six servings of fruits and vegetables be eaten each day.[1] Even for people who try to eat well, that's quite a challenge.

Spirulina complements the diets of all age groups. It is appropriate for the elderly, who are more likely than younger people to be deficient in certain nutrients and may not absorb, utilize, or store nutrients efficiently. Many elderly people are on medication for extended periods, which can interfere with nutrient levels. Because it may not be easy for them to get all their nutrition from food, spirulina becomes an ideal supplement, one that the body can easily digest and use. Spirulina is a high-energy food, and due to its soft cell wall, it is completely bioavailable.

"My husband, granddaughter and I have been taking Hawaiian Spirulina since 2011. The nutrient-rich Spirulina is good for, well, EVERYTHING. It means that we don't have to take an endless number of vitamins in a quest to discover what works and what doesn't. It doesn't replace food; it supplements it." — Dempsey Dybdahl, Seattle, WA

When there's not enough time to shop or cook, consuming spirulina means consuming "greens." This does not mean spirulina can salvage a junk food diet. To get the optimal health benefits, spirulina should be consumed alongside a nutritious diet and an active lifestyle. Children who won't eat their vegetables and students away from home are good candidates for adding spirulina to their diets, as are people who overconsume processed foods.

Pets and Plants

Not only do people enjoy the benefits of spirulina, but animals and plants can thrive on it, too. Veterinarians recommend spirulina for animal stamina and for general toning. Prize-winning koi carp are fed spirulina to enhance their color and health. Bird breeders add spirulina to bird food to enhance plumage color and luster. Spirulina is used extensively by aquaculture companies to increase disease resistance among various fish and shellfish and to improve their overall quality and coloration.[2]

Gardeners can use spirulina as a complete, effective plant food. Homeowners can sprinkle a little spirulina in the soil around their favorite houseplant and see what a difference it makes. Organic farmers can use spirulina as a natural fertilizer.

Why Take Spirulina?

Complete Protein

The protein in spirulina is complete, meaning that it contains all the essential amino acids. Spirulina also supplies non-essential amino acids. Non-essential does not mean that these amino acids are not needed by the body, but only that the body can produce them by itself. Still, the body is better served if they are readily available in dietary sources.

While most animal proteins are high in fat, calories, and cholesterol, a three-gram daily serving of spirulina has only five percent fat, most of which is unsaturated. There are fewer than four calories in each gram and practically no cholesterol.

Spirulina's protein is easily digested and assimilated. Other plants have cell walls of hard, indigestible cellulose, whereas spirulina's cell walls consist of soft mucopolysaccharides, making it easy for the body to digest. Digestibility and absorption are very important factors, especially for undernourished people, convalescents and the elderly.

To determine the percentage of usable protein in a food, the amount of protein present is measured along with its digestibility and biological value. As shown in Table 1.1, the only food with more usable protein than spirulina is eggs.

An Impressive Multivitamin and Mineral Source

Spirulina supplies several of the vitamins that all living beings need to carry on metabolic processes. These include all the B vitamins, including vitamin B12, the most difficult of all vitamins to obtain from vegetable sources. Hawaiian Spirulina contains 250 percent more of this rare vitamin than beef liver, previously thought to be the vitamin's richest source.

It also includes a substantial amount of vitamin A in the form of beta carotene. Vitamin A comes from two sources: animal sources and plants. Vitamin A from animal sources, called retinoids, can lead to toxicity levels. When it comes from plants it is called a carotenoid, which includes beta carotene. This is the form found in Hawaiian Spirulina. The body converts beta carotene to vitamin A as needed, without the concern of excess levels.

Vitamins K1 and K2 are found in spirulina, both of which play important roles in blood formation and circulation.

Few other microalgae contain the abundance of trace minerals, such as iron and zinc,

Table 1.1 Usable Protein Of Common Protein Foods[3]

Food	Protein (%)	NPU (%)*	Usable Protein (%)
Dried eggs	47	94	44
Spirulina	65	57	37
Dried skimmed milk	36	82	30
Soy flour	37	61	23
Fish	22	80	18
Chicken	24	67	16
Beef	22	67	16
Peanuts	26	38	10
* Net Protein Utilization			

and major minerals, such as potassium and magnesium, that Hawaiian Spirulina does.

Powerful Antioxidants

The potent trio of phytopigments found in spirulina can be found only in abundant quantities of fruits and vegetables. The yellow-orange carotenoids, the green chlorophyll, and the blue phycocyanin also make up the bulk of spirulina's antioxidant strength. Hawaiian Spirulina also contains superoxide dismutase (S.O.D.), one of the most powerful antioxidant enzymes. The importance of carotenoids, phycocyanin, and S.O.D. will be discussed in further detail in Chapter 2.

Essential Fatty Acids

Essential fatty acids, which include omega-6 and omega-3, are fats that the body cannot produce on its own, so they need to come from food sources. Omega-6s and omega-3s play a crucial role in supporting healthy brain function, as well as normal growth and development of cells. Spirulina is made up of about five percent lipids. These fats are absolutely vital to health.[4, 5]

Susan Smith Jones, Ph.D.

Little did I know that almost 30 years ago, when I first started taking Hawaiian Spiru-
lina, it would change my life. Hundreds of scientific studies have shown that spirulina
is the perfect high energy, low calorie, high protein, healing, alkalizing, detoxifying,
immune-system stimulating, and rejuvenating superfood for people of all ages.

I made a decision to try this wonder food that friends had been raving about to see if it
would make a difference for me. And what a positive and dramatic difference it made!
Within just one season—90 days—I slept like a baby, had energy to spare, could work
out longer and recuperate faster.

Over the decades, I've seen great healing occur with spirulina consumption both in
my private practice and with family members and friends dealing with cardiovascular
conditions. No coincidence here either: researchers have determined that spirulina is
a powerful antioxidant that helps to keep the circulatory and cardiovascular systems
running in top form.

Spirulina has also been scientifically proven to increase endurance, normalize aging,
detoxify the body (including the colon, skin, kidneys, and liver), protect the brain, and
neutralize free radicals.

I also appreciate that each serving of 3,000 mg of Hawaiian Spirulina has a whopping
270 mg of phycocyanin, the water-soluble blue pigment that gives spirulina its bluish
tint. It's one of the ingredients that makes the difference between spirulina and other
green foods like chlorella, wheat grass, and barley grass.

With its purity and potency, Hawaiian Spirulina is as good as it gets. Not only do I take
the tablets each day, especially when traveling, but I also enjoy adding the powder to
recipes. I have seen it cleanse, heal and rejuvenate countless people from the inside
out.

Dr. Susan Smith Jones is the author of 27 books including Walking on Air; The Joy
Factor; The Curative Kitchen; and Healthy, Happy & Radiant . . . at Any Age, plus over
2,000 magazine articles on these topics. Dr. Jones teaches that the body is designed
to be self-repairing, self-renewing, and self-sustaining and that the power to live a
radiantly healthy life is within everyone's grasp.

Figure 1.1 Typical Analysis of Hawaiian Spirulina*

Based on periodic analysis. Typical analysis per three grams – one teaspoon

General Composition

Protein	>60%
Carbohydrates	<30%
Lipids	4-6%
Minerals	8-13%
Moisture	3-6%
Calories	10

Minerals

Boron	22 mcg
Calcium	11 mg
Chromium	65 mcg
Copper	50 mcg
Iodine	15 mcg
Iron	5 mg
Magnesium	15 mg
Manganese	200 mcg
Phosphorus	30 mg
Potassium	43 mg
Selenium	0.9 mcg
Sodium	35 mg
Zinc	90 mcg

Vitamins

Biotin	0.5 mcg - < 1 mcg
Folic Acid	5 mcg
Inositol	1.7 mcg
Pantothenic Acid	5 mcg
Vitamin A (Beta Carotene)	9,500 IU
Vitamin B1 Thiamine	3 mcg
Vitamin B2 Riboflavin	179 mcg
Vitamin B3 Niacin	465 mcg
Vitamin B6 Pyridoxine	21 mcg
Vitamin B12 Cobalamin	8.0 mcg
Vitamin K1, K2	40 mcg

Phytonutrients

Chlorophyll	21 mg
Phycocyanin (c, allo)	270 mg
Zeaxanthin	3.0 mg
Total Carotenoids	13 mg

Hawaiian Spirulina also contains polysaccharides, enzymes (like Superoxide Dismutase), RNA, DNA, sulfolipids, glycogen, and many other potentially beneficial nutrients.

*Spirulina grown by Cyanotech Corporation on the pristine Kona Coast of Hawaii

Fatty Acids (Total 56.87 mg per gram)

Omega 3 Family
Alpha Linolenic	0.10 mg
Docosahexaenoic (DHA)	0.0435 mg

Omega 6 Family
Gamma Linolenic (GLA)	32 mg
Essential Linoleic	13.2 mg
Dihomogamma Linolenic	0.53 mg

Monoenoic Family
Palmitoleic	4.1 mg
Oleic	1.6 mg

Other Fatty Acids

Palmitic Acid	24.2 mg
Myristic Acid	0.10 mg
Stearic Acid	0.70 mg
Arachidonic Acid	0.10 mg

Protein

Spirulina is a superior source of dietary protein – about 60 percent highly digestible protein, containing all essential amino acids.

Typical Amino Acid Analysis

Essential Amino Acids	Percent of Total	Mg per Gram
Isoleucine	5.98	34.6
Leucine	8.91	51.6
Lysine	4.99	28.9
Methionine	2.47	14.3
Phenylalanine	4.98	28.8
Threonine	5.25	30.4
Tryptophan	1.80	10.4
Valine	6.00	34.7
Non-Essential Amino Acids		
Alanine	7.90	45.7
Arginine	7.31	42.3
Aspartic Acid	10.14	58.7
Cystine	0.97	5.6
Glutamic Acid	13.94	80.7
Glycine	5.44	31.5
Histidine	1.77	10.4
Proline	4.01	23.6
Serine	4.89	28.8
Tyrosine	4.74	28.2
Total	**100.0**	**589.0**

Please Note: This is only a partial list of the variety of health-giving nutrients found in Hawaiian Spirulina.

How Much Spirulina Should Be Taken and When?

Research supports adults taking three grams of spirulina daily for overall health. Children only need one to two grams per day depending on their body weight. Clinical trials have evaluated spirulina doses up to 10 grams daily with no side effects, and many active people prefer to take larger amounts. Spirulina may be taken in tablet or powder form. Both are equally beneficial.

Spirulina may be taken with or without food, and can be taken at one time or various times throughout the day. Spirulina increases energy levels in most people, so it's best to take it at least four hours before going to bed.

Chapter

2

The Synergy of Nine Potent Nutrients

Spirulina is the supreme example of synergy. Although each nutrient has its own nutritional and therapeutic power, together they assist each other in ways they cannot do alone. That is why it is important to experience the synergy of Hawaiian Spirulina by consuming it as a whole food, rather than relying on its individual extracts.

Spirulina is composed of both fat-soluble and water-soluble nutrients. Both types can be found on the shelves as individual extracts, but their value is limited if they are not consumed together. The aqueous interior of cells, for example, needs water-soluble nutrients, like phycocyanin. And the lipid cell walls of the brain, for example, need fat-soluble nutrients like beta carotene.

Hawaiian Spirulina, the brand produced on the Big Island of Hawaii by Cyanotech and distributed by Nutrex Hawaii, is the pride of the Pacific. Because it is grown in such an idyllic environment, it can retain more of its nutrients from pond to package than other brands. Therefore, when this book refers to the nutrients in spirulina, it's referring to the nutrients in the Hawaiian Spirulina brand.

Hawaiian Spirulina makes available in one teaspoon what five servings of fruits and vegetables provide. The nine key nutrients of Hawaiian Spirulina elevate it to superfood status. They are:

- Phycocyanin
- Beta carotene
- Zeaxanthin
- Iron
- Vitamin B12
- Vitamin K
- GLA (gamma linolenic acid)
- Trace minerals
- S.O.D. (superoxidase dismutase)

❶ Phycocyanin: The Power of "Blue" in Blue-Green Microalgae

Phycocyanin (*phyco* meaning "algae" and *cyanin* meaning "blue-green") is a powerful molecule only found in spirulina and some other blue-green algae. It is a water-soluble antioxidant and gives spirulina its rich blue-green pigment. Spirulina is the only whole food that contains this blue antioxidant. Wheat grass and chlorella are green from chlorophyll, but only spirulina has both the blue *and* green antioxidants.

Phycocyanin, a water-soluble protein, works with the chlorophyll in Hawaiian Spirulina to become a powerful antioxidant. Scientists have labeled phycocyanin "a wonder molecule" for its many health benefits.[6] Phycocyanin has been shown to:

- Maintain healthy liver and kidney function
- Support the immune system
- Protect brain tissue
- Promote the detoxification of radioactive substances and metals from the body
- Help to normalize aging of the skin.

❷ Beta carotene: The Antioxidant for Skin, Eyes, and Immune System

Beta carotene is one of the most important antioxidants for skin, eyes, and immune function. It belongs to the family of fat-soluble antioxidants called carotenoids, the nutrients responsible for the bright orange and yellow color of pumpkins, carrots, and sweet potatoes. Beta carotene is a precursor of vitamin A. The body converts the carotenoid to vitamin A to protect cells from oxidization. Vitamin A behaves like a scavenger of oxidized cells in the body. When sunlight, for example, causes skin cells to oxidize, vitamin A, working in tandem with other vitamins and minerals in Hawaiian Spirulina, can latch onto those cells, protecting them from further breakdown. It also contributes to skin health and radiant appearance and works with other antioxidants to protect the cornea of the eye and boost the immune system.

Table 2.1 Beta carotene in Food Comparison[7]

Food	Amount of Beta Carotene
Hawaiian Spirulina (three grams)	9,500 IU
Carrot, small (50 grams)	8,353 IU
Papaya, large (781 grams)	7,420 IU
Pumpkin, 1 cup raw (116 grams)	9,875 IU
Chlorella (three grams)	845 IU

❸ Zeaxanthin: The Antioxidant for the Retina, Lens, and Brain Tissue

Zeaxanthin is also part of the carotenoid family of antioxidants. Like beta carotene, it is found in brightly colored fruits and vegetables. Zeaxanthin specifically works on the retina and lens of the eyes. Zeaxanthin protects the eyes by absorbing damaging blue light and reducing glare. Over time, blue light can cause oxidative stress in the eyes.[8] Zeaxanthin's antioxidant properties naturally reduce these harmful effects

In the side-by-side antioxidant test shown in Figure 2.1, zeaxanthin came out almost 500 times stronger than vitamin E. The only antioxidant that was more powerful in quenching singlet oxygen, the highly unstable form of oxygen responsible for oxidation damage, was astaxanthin.

The ability of zeaxanthin to cross the blood-brain barrier to fight the oxidative degeneration of brain tissue is another reason to consume zeaxanthin.

Food and dietary supplements are the only way to get zeaxanthin in the bloodstream, because it is not made naturally in the body.[9] Receiving adequate amounts of zeaxanthin through food can be particularly difficult, as it requires many servings a day of certain fruits and vegetables. A three-gram serving of Hawaiian Spirulina has more zeaxanthin than a bowl of spinach, one of nature's richest sources of zeaxanthin.

Figure. 2.1 Singlet Oxygen Quenching Rates[10]

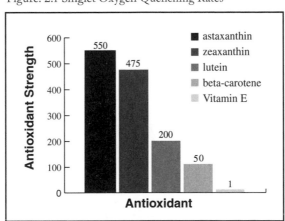

❹ Iron: For Richer Blood and Energy

Hawaiian Spirulina has by far the highest levels of iron of any brand of spirulina. Iron is an essential element for life on earth, primarily for its role in producing blood. About 70 percent of the body's iron is found in red blood cells and muscle cells. Red blood cells transfer oxygen from the lungs to all the cells in the body. The immune system especially depends on available iron stores.[11]

Iron is also involved in the conversion of blood sugar to energy. Metabolic energy is crucial for athletes since it allows muscles to work at their optimum levels during exercise or when competing.

Vegetarians, especially, are prone to iron deficiency, since iron is most commonly found in meats. Because the body recognizes spirulina as a food and spirulina's cell walls are perfectly digestible, the iron in spirulina is easily absorbed. This makes Hawaiian Spirulina an ideal source of iron: five milligrams of iron in a three-gram serving of Hawaiian Spirulina make up 30 percent of the U.S. Food and Drug Administration recommended daily value (see Figure 2.2).

Figure 2.2 Iron Content of Spirulina

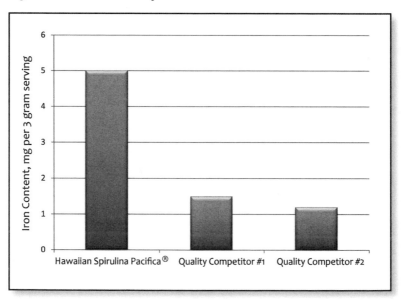

Source: Cyanotech Corporation

⑤ Vitamin B12: For Vegetarians and Vegans

Vitamin B12 has a key role in the normal functioning of the nervous system and the formation of blood. Vegetarians and vegans are susceptible to being vitamin B12 deficient, because the vitamin is mostly found in animals and animal products. The foods with the highest amounts of vitamin B12 are cooked clams, beef liver, and mackerel. Vegetarians and vegans have to find a way to get this essential vitamin into their diets. Fortunately, one daily serving of three grams of Hawaiian Spirulina gives 150 percent of the recommended daily value of vitamin B12.

There are two different kinds of vitamin B12: human-active, which the body can absorb and use; and analog which is not absorbed by the body. Both forms are found in Hawaiian Spirulina. The amount of human-active B12 represents 54 percent of the U.S. FDA recommended daily intake of B12. (The analog B12 does not interfere with the absorption of human-active B12, and neither form has side effects or toxicity.)

⑥ Vitamin K: For Arterial and Bone Health

While the health benefits of vitamins A, B, C, D, and E are widely known, the benefits of vitamin K are still emerging, and there are many. Most important, this fat-soluble vitamin plays a role in blood clotting. In fact, the K comes from the German word *koagulation*. Its particular chemistry also promotes decalcification of the arteries. Vitamin K has also been studied for its role in preserving bone mineral density, especially in the elderly. [12, 13]

Vitamin K has two main forms, K1 and K2. K2 is suggested to be the form of vitamin K most responsible for maintaining healthy cardiovascular function. A three-gram daily serving of Hawaiian Spirulina provides 50 percent of the U.S. FDA recommended daily dose of vitamin K. A tremendous amount of leafy green vegetables would have to be consumed to get the same dose.

⑦ GLA: Essential Fatty Acid for the Brain

Gamma-linolenic acid (GLA) is an omega-6 fatty acid that is found mostly in hard-to-find plant oils, like evening primrose oil. The oils in Hawaiian Spirulina contain three times more GLA than what is found in evening primrose oil. Omega-6 fatty acids are considered essential fatty acids: While they are necessary for human health, the body must supply them from food. Along with omega-3 fatty acids, omega-6 fatty acids have a powerful antioxidant effect on brain tissue, protecting the brain from cognitive decline due to oxidative deterioration. These antioxidants are also known for their protection of the arteries, skin, and bones, as well as their role in metabolism and reproduction.

⑧ Trace Minerals: Deep-Ocean Source

Every second of every day, the body relies on trace minerals to conduct and generate billions of tiny electrical impulses. Without these impulses, not a single muscle, including the heart, would be able to function. The brain would not function and the cells would not be able to use osmosis to balance water pressure and absorb nutrients. Traditionally, eating fresh grains, fruits, and vegetables grown in nutrient-rich soil has been the primary supply for a full spectrum of minerals. Unfortunately, in today's world, naturally occurring, nutrient-rich soil is becoming increasingly rare. Eons of vegetation growth and aggressive modern farming techniques have brought many of the earth's minerals to the surface where they have been washed away into the ocean.

Hawaiian Spirulina is grown in ponds that are enriched with a small percentage of deep sea water pumped from 2,000 feet below the ocean's surface. This is where the trace minerals such as iron, zinc, copper, iodine, selenium, manganese, chromium, fluoride, and molybdenum have settled. Spirulina absorbs these minerals into its delicate filaments and makes them available in the human body, where they work to create and restore health.

❾ S.O.D.: The Antioxidant Catalyst

The enzyme superoxide dismutase, or S.O.D, has been called the "antioxidant catalyst," because it speeds up the breakdown of superoxide radicals produced as a byproduct of energy metabolism. If not regulated, superoxide radicals cause many types of cellular damage.

The benefits of S.O.D. in normalizing aging have been widely demonstrated. A University of California, San Diego, study reported that "[S.O.D.] protects cells from toxic, reactive oxygen species and may be involved in age-related degeneration." [14] In Finland, scientists concluded "compounds with S.O.D. and catalase activities have shown promising results in animal models against a variety of oxidant exposures." [15] At the University of Colorado School of Medicine, researchers found that the space between individual cells is protected from oxidative stress by S.O.D. and that this activity is more highly pronounced in blood vessels, the heart, lungs, kidneys, and the placenta. [16]

Although S.O.D. is one the more important antioxidants the body relies on, the enzyme is susceptible to the harsh acids present in the human stomach. As a result of a patented ocean chill drying method, the S.O.D. in Hawaiian Spirulina tablets is not highly destroyed by stomach acids, which can be a potential problem when taking S.O.D. in some supplement forms.

But what about Hawaiian Spirulina powder? Will stomach acids destroy the S.O.D. before it can get into the bloodstream if spirulina is taken in powder form? Research suggests that even powder sources of S.O.D. elevate S.O.D. levels in the body. [17]

Not many foods qualify as a complete source of nutrition. The label of superfood is reserved for only an elite few. The antioxidants, vitamins, and minerals found in Hawaiian Spirulina can each stand alone in their importance to human health. But when one food can deliver all of them in rich supply and with a synergy that empowers them to greater effectiveness, their impact is multiplied and their contributions to health unparalleled.

Chapter

3

Superfood for Super Health

The combination of nutrients in Hawaiian Spirulina is what elevates this blue-green microalgae to superfood status. A three-gram serving provides many of the nutrients necessary for optimal health. Scientists have widely studied the health benefits of spirulina, and their results have been published in peer-reviewed journals around the world. Although many of the studies reported here were conducted in a laboratory, they are being joined by a growing number of clinical trials and both types of study results consistently agree on spirulina's health attributes.

- Sustained energy
- Year-round immune support
- Heavy metal and radiation reduction
- Antioxidant benefits
- Essential iron source
- Brain cell support
- Liver and kidney support
- Cardiovascular health maintenance

Sustained Energy

People consume staggering amounts of coffee and other caffeinated drinks for one main purpose – to give themselves an artificial energy boost to get through the day. The body is perfectly capable of supplying its own energy so long as it stays in optimal working order. Overeating processed foods, sitting too long at a desk, lack of sleep, and other detriments to health deplete the body's natural energy reserves.

Assuming lifestyle changes are on most people's to-do list, supplementing with Hawaiian Spirulina offers a kind of shortcut to health. With the synergy of its beta carotene, iron, vitamins, phycocyanin, and other nutrients, Hawaiian Spirulina can provide sustained energy without the crash. And because it is a natural food, there are no chemicals to counteract the health benefits.

In 2006, a small double-blind, placebo-controlled study was conducted on non-athletic male and female university students to test their endurance and energy levels. Each student took 2.5 grams of spirulina or a placebo before each meal, for a total of 7.5 grams per day. The students' blood was measured at the beginning and at the end of the study and they were tested on a treadmill to see how long they could run until they became exhausted. After three weeks, with no other changes in their diet or exercise, the students taking spirulina lasted 7.3 percent longer on the treadmill before becoming exhausted. And the oxidative stress levels in their blood went down by 25 percent.[18]

Another small study was conducted on nine men of the average age of 23, but in this study they were moderately athletic and were consistently training.[19] This double-blind, placebo-controlled study had the treatment group taking six grams of spirulina each day for four weeks. Scientists found that spirulina users tired less quickly, burned more fats, and improved their total antioxidant capacity (alongside other markers of health). These moder-

"I have always been very active and speed walk or cycle at least an hour every day for the last forty years. As I have gotten older I have noticed that I am more tired when finished and don't recuperate as fast. Enter Hawaiian Spirulina. I am amazed by how much more energy I have now. It's almost like a miracle has taken place in my life." — Cliff Alexander, Bonita Springs, FL

Figure 3.1   Increased Endurance[20]

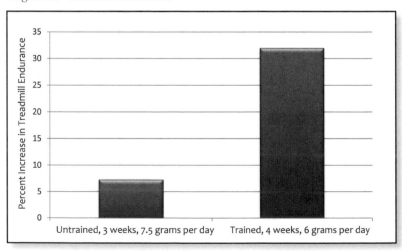

ately athletic men's endurance increased by 32 percent versus only seven percent in the first study (see Figure 3.1).

Year-Round Immune Support

If the human body could stay strong and responsive each day, life could be enjoyed to the fullest. Immune systems would be supported all year round. Hawaiian Spirulina's combination of nutrients is like a net to an acrobat, always there should the immune system take a fall. Medical research continues to find that spirulina supports a healthy immune system. In fact, improved immunity and increased energy are the number one and two health benefits that Hawaiian Spirulina consumers report.

"Spirulina is my go-to immune system booster. I take it with me while traveling, during allergy season, and during stressful time periods." — Julie Morris, Superfoods Chef, Los Angeles, Calif.

Many people claim that after starting daily use of Hawaiian Spirulina, their energy has improved and they feel healthier. A survey of nearly 200 Hawaiian Spirulina users adds some anecdotal evidence to this phenomenon.[21] The survey was conducted on a variety of consumers. Their use of spirulina differed in how much spirulina they consumed and how often. For example:

- 15 percent had not taken spirulina for over a month at the time they took the survey.
- 16 percent had been using spirulina for less than two months.
- 30 percent had been using it for less than six months.
- 31 percent were using spirulina only one to five days a week (recommendation on the label is for daily use).
- 27 percent were not using the recommended three grams a day.

Although these consumers had very different usage patterns, almost 77 percent of them reported that their immune systems had improved since starting on Hawaiian Spirulina. And 80 percent of them reported that they had more energy. Again, surveys such as this one are anecdotal but do suggest the positive benefits of supplementing with spirulina.

Eric Gershwyn, a medical doctor and University of California, Davis, professor, founded the Allergy and Clinical Immunology Program at the university in 1977. As an expert in the immune system, he has studied spirulina's role in reinforcing the body's immune system. In one study, Gershwyn looked at the immune system of 40 healthy men and women over age 50 who had no history of chronic disease. He gave each of them three grams of Hawaiian Spirulina tablets over 12 weeks. He found that the two immunity markers used to measure immune strength – white blood cell count and certain liver enzymes – increased in the majority of subjects,[22] demonstrating spirulina's positive role in bolstering the immune system.

In 2002, researchers in Mexico and Russia independently observed spirulina's reinforcing effect on immune cells compromised by infection in a laboratory setting.[23, 24] They found that spirulina demonstrated antiviral activity by inhibiting cells from becoming infected by certain viruses and by slowing the reproduction of certain viruses.

Heavy Metal and Radiation Reduction

The filamentous, soft mucopolysaccharide walls that define blue-green microalgae act like cotton in a dish of water. They soak up the water surrounding them. The fibers that make up the mucopolysaccharides also have the ability to bind toxins, especially heavy metals such as mercury and lead. Spirulina acts essentially like tiny brooms, sweeping the toxins away and safely disposing them.

In many developing countries, tap water contains high levels of heavy metals and other toxins. Scientists have experimented with spirulina and zinc to determine whether people exposed to toxins in the drinking water were better equipped to handle the harmful effects after they were given the microalgae–zinc combination. After 16 weeks, overall reduced toxicity was observed.[25] Similar results were seen in a study of laboratory rats exposed to high levels of lead. Spirulina helped the rats to detoxify the lead levels in their brains.[26] And because spirulina is full of antioxidants, the tissues of the brain were more resilient to oxidative damage.[27-30]

In 1986, a nuclear power plant in Chernobyl, Ukraine, exploded and exposed the residents living nearby to extremely high radiation levels. Scientists validated the exposure by measuring the radioactive substances in the residents' urine samples. Knowing spirulina's propensity to bind toxins to its mucopolysaccharide walls, scientists administered five grams of spirulina to the children in the area. After six months, the radiation levels in the children's

---

Hawaiian Spirulina Is Completely Free of Radiation from Fukushima, Japan

Since the 2011 nuclear disaster in Fukushima, Japan, consumers have been concerned about radiation contamination in the Pacific Ocean. Hawaiian Spirulina is grown in fresh drinking water with a small amount of deep ocean water added in. Hawaiian Spirulina has been regularly tested for radiation by independent labs. The results have consistently found Hawaiian Spirulina to be 100 percent free of any detectable radioactivity.

urine were reduced by 50 percent.[31]

Antioxidant Benefits

Antioxidants have a tough job. Like the Greek myth of Sisyphus, who repeatedly pushed a boulder uphill only to have it roll down again, antioxidants must stay strong enough to keep the free radicals from rolling through the body, breaking down tissue in their wake.

The outward signs of free radical damage are lines, wrinkles, and dry skin, for example. Internally, free radicals impair muscle tissue, cardiovascular tissue, brain tissue, and other organ tissues. On a cellular level, free radicals can damage DNA, leading to a faster than normal rate of aging.

Although spirulina looks primarily green, it actually contains four distinct pigments, each of which is known for its antioxidant power on different parts of the body, though they often overlap.

- Green: chlorophyll (for detoxification)
- Orange: beta carotene (for skin, eyes, and immune system)
- Yellow: zeaxanthin (for eyes and brain)
- Blue: phycocyanin (for liver, kidneys, brain, and immunity).[32]

Spirulina also contains superoxide dismutase, or S.O.D., an antioxidant enzyme that supplements the body's natural stores of S.O.D.

Many antioxidant extracts are either water-soluble or fat-soluble. But spirulina contains both kinds. Its antioxidants beta carotene and zeaxanthin are fat-soluble, giving them the advantage of crossing the fatty cell membranes. Whereas the water-soluble phycocyanin, chlorophyll, and S.O.D. can be used in the more watery centers of the cell.

Compared to chlorella, another healthful microalgae, spirulina has five times the antioxidant strength and an overall antioxidant activity that's about 30 percent higher. And it has been demonstrated that spirulina has a stronger protective effect on human liver cells in laboratory settings than chlorella does.[33]

Essential Iron Source

An essential mineral means that the body can't manufacture it on its own and must get it from food. One of the most essential minerals in the body is iron. Without it, blood cells (hemoglobin) and muscle cells would be unable to deliver oxygen. Spirulina is a naturally rich source of iron. The body is able to absorb more iron from spirulina than from other mineral-rich foods such as beef. Researchers in Montpellier, France, found that consumption of spirulina led to iron bioavailability that was 6.5 times higher than from consumption of beef.[34]

A study in Calcutta, India, compared two randomly divided groups of women: one that received only a supplement of iron, folic acid, and B12, and another that received spirulina along with that supplement. The study found that the addition of spirulina to the supplement resulted in the women having higher hemoglobin levels than without the spirulina.[35]

Healthy stores of iron and the resulting increased hemoglobin are particularly important to women who are pregnant or breastfeeding. In an animal study, researchers found that spirulina improved the amount of hemoglobin and iron storage in rats that were either pregnant or lactating. The improvement was compared to diets of fortified plant sources of iron, namely casein and wheat gluten.[36]

Ascorbic acid, or vitamin C, plays a key role in enhancing iron absorption in the body. Even with the rich source of iron in spirulina, it is important to also consume oranges, strawberries, broccoli, and other foods with vitamin C. Hawaiian Spirulina has a healthy amount of vitamin B12 and folic acid, both of which help the body absorb iron.

Brain Cell Support

In a roomful of fruits and vegetables, why do blueberries consistently get all the attention? The answer, of course, is because of its rich antioxidant content. But this knowledge wasn't widely known until Dr. Paula Bickford, a professor in the Department of Neurosurgery at the University of South Florida College of Medicine, conducted extensive research on the health benefits of eating blueberries. Her findings were so well publicized that she was able to establish blueberries as a superfood.

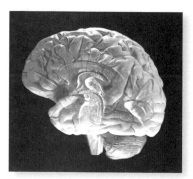

After this work, she turned her attention to spirulina. Specifically, she studied spirulina's effects on the brain. In a comparison study of the effects of spirulina, blueberries, and spinach on the brain health of laboratory rats, in which some rats were fed spirulina, some rats blueberries, some rats spinach, and some rats a control food that contained none of the above, she found that the rats that were fed a daily diet of either of the three antioxidant-rich foods for four weeks showed sustained levels of heightened cognition. Spirulina, especially, had significant positive outcomes on the brain scans of rats.[37]

She also studied spirulina's effect on stem cell proliferation. A daily dose of spirulina was administered to laboratory rats for 30 days. Stem cells are important for learning and memory, essentially a repair system in the human body. They can divide in unlimited numbers to replenish other cells. She found that "a diet enriched with spirulina and other nutraceuticals may help protect the stem/progenitor cells from insults."[38] This means that Hawaiian Spirulina may support the brain's ability to withstand deterioration.

Although these results have yet to be demonstrated in human clinical trials, the animal trials have consistently found several potential neurological benefits from taking spi-

Professor Paula Bickford, Ph.D.

I first started taking spirulina because my acupuncturist suggested that it might help me with my fatigue. After a short time, I did begin to feel better and have been taking spirulina regularly ever since. It was not until several years later, after I had started doing research on blueberries and other fruits and vegetables, that I thought about doing research on spirulina. I was living in Colorado at the time and was on vacation up in the mountains on a sort of work/meditation retreat. One morning I woke up and was drinking my green drink with spirulina and realized that I needed to study spirulina in my research.

As soon as I got back to my lab, I asked my lab manager to run spirulina on the ORAC test, which is a test that determines the antioxidant activity of various compounds. For this particular test a chemical is used that when it gets oxidized (attacked by free radicals), it loses fluorescence, which we can detect on a machine. We put the spirulina into the test solution and waited for the fluorescence signal to go down. Usually for blueberry this took about an hour. With spirulina, six hours later we were still waiting and waiting. As it turned out, the antioxidant activity of spirulina was the highest of anything we ever tested before that time. Then I knew that we had to test spirulina some more. That began my long-term interest in studying the biological effects of spirulina.

Paula C. Bickford, Ph.D., is a Professor of Neurosurgery and Brain Repair at the University of South Florida and Senior Research Career scientist at James A. Haley VA Hospital in Tampa, Florida. Dr. Bickford is one of the leading researchers in the field of aging and is a past president of the American Aging Association and the American Society of Neural Therapy and Repair. Dr. Bickford is a personal fan of Hawaiian Spirulina and has published groundbreaking research on spirulina including four pre-clinical trials showing a variety of potential benefits for brain health.

rulina. Simply put, all signs point to spirulina being a neuroprotective supplement. Many other scientists continue to study how exactly spirulina supports the brain. They have found in laboratories that spirulina promotes lead detoxification,[39] improves motor functioning,[40] and protects the brain from oxidative stress. [41-45]

Liver and Kidney Support

The liver and kidneys are responsible for turning food into energy and safely ridding unwanted by-products. The body's own antioxidants enable the cells of the liver and kidneys to do their job without breaking down from exposure to free radicals.

Free radicals are the name of unstable oxygen molecules that are formed during normal metabolism and exposure to environmental stressors, such as strenuous exercise, air and water pollution, chemicals in foods, and multiple sources of radiation, including sunlight.

When the body's antioxidants can't keep up with the number of free radicals, the liver and kidneys are unable to perform at necessary rates.

This is where spirulina comes in. The antioxidant array of vitamins, minerals, and phytonutrients in spirulina is immediately recruited to the areas of the body that are losing the battle against free radicals. In several studies around the world, scientists tested spirulina's antioxidant effect on the liver and kidneys by exposing rats to a known oxidant and observing whether spirulina can bolster the liver and kidney cells' ability to withstand oxidation. The results unilaterally showed a positive correlation between spirulina and the function of liver and kidney cells.[46-52]

Cardiovascular Health Benefits

When a food is said to be good for the heart, it usually means it's good for the cardiovascular system. The heart might be the hardest-working organ in the body, but it doesn't work alone. To do its job, it depends on the arteries to carry nutrient-rich blood to all the areas of the body. And it depends on veins to return the depleted blood back to the heart. The antioxidant concentration in Hawaiian Spirulina, especially that in phycocyanin, is designed to cooperate alongside this system. Phycocyanin is known for its protective activity on heart cells and the cells lining the blood vessels.[53] Its presence helps prevent the cells from oxidizing.

In a human clinical trial in Mexico, scientists administered 4.5 grams a day of spirulina to 36 subjects and measured several cardiovascular indicators before and after the spirulina intake.[54] The group was a diverse mix of men and women ages 18 to 65. They were told to go about their lives without any dietary restrictions. After six weeks of consuming spirulina, scientists discovered that their systolic and diastolic blood pressure had lowered.

In another human clinical trial, conducted in Korea on 78 healthy, elderly men and women ages 60 to 87, scientists wanted to test spirulina's nutritive effects on the cardiovascular system. The men and women were given either eight grams of spirulina a day or a placebo,

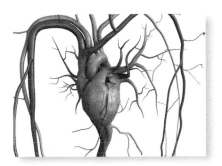

Human heart and connecting blood vessels

for 16 weeks. The scientists found, "Spirulina has favorable effects on lipid profiles, immune variables, and antioxidant capacity in healthy, elderly males and females and is suitable as a functional food."[55] Cardiovascular function is compromised when blood flow is reduced by unhealthy lipid levels. The addition of spirulina to the diets of these men and women promoted optimal lipid levels, which in turn benefited cardiovascular function.

While more studies on humans are needed to validate these results, the consistent findings suggest that consuming spirulina for cardiovascular health makes heart sense.

Chapter

4

High-Quality Spirulina Production and Environmental Stewardship

A pioneer in microalgae production, Cyanotech has been growing superior spirulina for over 30 years. The company has a reputation of excellence in the extra care and attention it pays to the growing, harvesting, and processing of Hawaiian Spirulina. Furthermore, the Cyanotech team is steadfast in its commitment to sustainability in order to create a cleaner, safer, and healthier world.

The methods to ensure that Hawaiian Spirulina production meets the highest-possible standards range from a patented drying system to vacuum-sealed and light-protected packaging, all performed with the goal of continually reducing the company's carbon footprint.

Ocean Chill Drying™

Cyanotech has developed a proprietary drying method called Ocean Chill Drying™ that uses cold ocean water pumped from 2,000 feet below the surface of the Pacific Ocean. The ocean water cools and dehumidifies the warm moist air exiting the dryer. The dehumidified air is then recycled back into the dryer. As air recycles through the dryer, the oxygen level drops to less than one percent and carbon dioxide increases and gets recycled into the spirulina ponds. Not only is this an environmentally responsible drying method, but it is a way to keep oxygen to a minimum in the drying process. If the antioxidants in spirulina are exposed to oxygen, they will oxidize and become ineffective. The harvesting process of Hawaiian Spirulina is so efficient that the spirulina goes from pond culture to finished product in less than 30 minutes, which reduces its exposure to oxygen and preserves its nutrients.

Tests have been run with and without Ocean Chill Drying. Without it, as much as 50 to 60 percent of the antioxidants in spirulina

Figure 4.1 Ocean Chill Drying Process

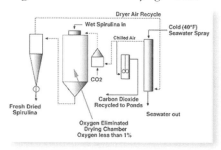

Source: Cyanotech

are neutralized. Data from independent laboratories, in fact, show antioxidants present in Hawaiian Spirulina that are not present in other brands.[56]

Triple Rinse Process

Hawaiian Spirulina is rinsed at least three times before being dried. In addition, the facility shuts down every day for four to five hours for an intense cleaning. Cyanotech's dedication to hygienic production not only removes contaminants that might oxidize S.O.D. and other fragile nutrients, but also leaves Hawaiian Spirulina with a fresher taste than could otherwise be achieved.

S.O.D. Preservation

One of the consequences of an inferior manufacturing process is a low level of S.O.D. in the final product. The tendency of S.O.D. to break down makes S.O.D. the ideal nutrient to measure when comparing spirulina brands. If the brand contains a high level of S.O.D., it means the company's manufacturing methods passed muster. Conversely, a low level of S.O.D. means something in the production line did not meet quality control. Hawaiian Spirulina has more S.O.D. in every three grams than other brands.

Pure Drinking Water

Hawaiian Spirulina is grown using 100 percent pure drinking water from the Big Island's pristine aquifer, which collects water that has been filtered through lava rock to maximize its purity. The majority of the fresh water is recycled back to the spirulina pond for the next growing cycle to reduce water waste. The potable-water ponds are infused with a very small percentage of deep ocean water to expose the absorptive microalgae to the deep ocean's abundant mineral content.

Continuous Culture System

A continuous culture system means that only about 70 percent of the Hawaiian Spirulina culture is harvested at a time, with the remaining microalgae left behind to re-seed the next batch. This allows for a continuous infusion of nutrients from harvest to harvest. Because Hawaiian Spirulina has been cultivated in this way for over 30 years, it has evolved into a superior strain. The continuous culture depends on Hawaii's year-round ideal climate to ensure that there are no interruptions in the growing cycle.

BioSecure Zone

Hawaiian Spirulina is grown in a BioSecure zone, where it is illegal to use genetically modified organisms (also known as GMOs) or other contaminants. The remote and pristine Kona coast is far from any agricultural operations that use pesticides and synthetic fertilizers.

Cold-Pressed Tableting

Hawaiian Spirulina tablets are cold-pressed to avoid exposing the spirulina to the high heat used in traditional tableting methods. Just as with overcooking vegetables, subjecting spirulina to high heat destroys many of the vitamins, minerals, and antioxidants the food is known for. Cold-pressing spirulina also reduces electricity consumption and so is a more environmentally conscious method than using heat.

Strict Quality Control from Pond to Package

Cyanotech reviews and measures every stage of Hawaiian Spirulina production from cultivation to harvest. Seventeen separate quality tests are conducted to ensure that the spirulina meets strict specifications, including measuring the levels of each nutrient and testing for heavy metal contamination. The facility regularly undergoes third-party Good Manufacturing Practices (GMP) inspections, processing inspections, and other quality-control tests.

Once the spirulina has passed the rigorous testing, the bulk product is packaged and distributed worldwide. The raw spirulina is contained in a foil bag that serves as an oxygen barrier. An oxygen absorber is placed in each bag, the air is vacuumed out, and the bag is heat-sealed and placed in a sturdy cardboard box. The great care to remove all oxygen and prevent exposure to light during shipping and storage protects spirulina's fragile nutrients. To ensure that the quality packaging is continued from bulk to finished consumer goods, Cyanotech launched Nutrex Hawaii in 1990 to oversee all areas of consumer marketing and packaging.

Environmental Responsibility and Stewardship

Spirulina is one of the world's most environmentally efficient crops. It produces 20 times more protein per acre than common crops such as corn and soybeans, and uses 10 times less water in the farming.

Figure 4.2 Gallons of Water Used to Produce One Pound of Protein

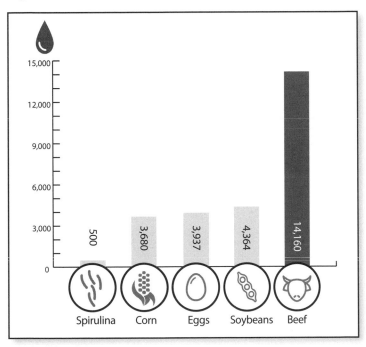

Source: Cyanotech

Cyanotech also uses cold deep seawater to save energy. The company utilizes water that is pumped up from 2,000 feet below the surface of the Pacific Ocean to cool its ponds and run its Ocean Chill Drying process as explained earlier in this chapter. The cold seawater is also as a source of air conditioning for Cyanotech's offices. By running pipes through its buildings, the company is able to bring in the cold water, efficiently and effectively cooling its offices with low energy usage.

To further reduce its carbon footprint, Cyanotech recently added 2,280 solar array panels, which produce 1,147,000 kilowatt-hours of electricity each year. The energy production is sufficient to power the farms during daylight hours, with projected greenhouse gas emissions reduced by 791 metric tons of carbon dioxide per year—that's equivalent to the annual greenhouse gas emissions of 167 passenger vehicles.

Chapter

5

Better Than Organic

Q: Is it best to eat organic vegetables, fruits, and other foods?
A: Yes

Q: Is it best to eat organic spirulina?
A: No

All living organisms need food to survive, and the principal food that spirulina needs is nitrogen. For over three billion years, spirulina has grown wildly in soda lakes and relied on the rich, inorganic minerals of the lakebed soil, which include nitrogen and phosphorus. Hawaiian Spirulina is cultured in ponds off the Kona coast of Hawaii. The same growing conditions found in nature billions of years ago are recreated in these ponds to cultivate the purest form of spirulina today.

Unlike Hawaiian Spirulina, most cultivated spirulina is grown with synthetic nitrogen made from petrochemicals. This nitrogen source can be purchased easily and cheaply. Cyanotech, alternatively, uses a chemical-free, natural source of nitrogen that is mined from the deep earth. Nitrogen-laden deep rock has fed spirulina lakes long before spirulina became commercialized. Cyanotech lines its ponds and cultivates its spirulina in a self-contained ecosystem, guaranteeing no runoff and no soil contamination. Mined nitrogen from the deep earth is the highest-quality source a grower can use.

In 2005, the U.S. Department of Agriculture's National Organics Standards Board (NOSB) ruled that all-natural, mined nitrogen from the earth is not allowable in organic foods. The NOSB allows only two alternatives, both of which are organic and both of which carry health risks. These are fertilizers from animal manure and fertilizers from decomposed plants (also called compost teas). Cyanotech has examined these sources of nitrogen and found them to be unsatisfactory for Hawaiian Spirulina because they could:

- Contaminate the microalgae with lead and other heavy metals
- Increase the bacterial count
- Deplete the nutrients

To be absolutely certain that it was making the right choice in giving up its organic certification, Cyanotech conducted independent research on these alternative sources of nitrogen. A reputable spirulina producer in California, called Earthrise, had also been faced with the decision on whether to keep its organic label and begin using animal manure or compost teas. Earthrise also conducted independent research.

After analyzing the results, both companies came to the same conclusion. Organic sources of nitrogen would compromise the quality and safety of spirulina. The highly absorptive microalgae could potentially soak up the bacteria and heavy metals that could be present in animal manure and compost teas. This exposure to cow manure or decomposed organic matter would also spoil spirulina's taste and smell. Finally, spirulina grown in these conditions would be depleted of some of its most prized, but fragile, nutrients.

Table 5.1 Natural vs. Organic Spirulina

Comparison -	All Natural U.S. Grown Spirulina	"Organic" Spirulina Produced Under the New Standard
Pesticide Free	✓	✓
Herbicide Free	✓	✓
Environmentally Friendly	✓	✓
Purified Nutrients	✓	
Low Bacterial Count	✓	
Low Heavy Metal Level	✓	
Non-Animal Fertilizers	✓	
Minimally Processed	✓	
Higher Growth Rate	✓	

Source: Cyanotech

Both Cyanotech and Earthrise chose the health and safety of its consumers over the much more lucrative "organic" label. Despite the fear that consumers' preference for organic food would cut Cyanotech from the market, the company went forward with is all-natural labels. Cyanotech was rewarded for its economic bravery. No loss of market share or sales has occurred as a result of the new labeling. In fact, in the U.S. market, Hawaiian Spirulina has nearly 50 percent of all spirulina sales.

Because Hawaiian Spirulina continues to use natural nitrogen mined from the earth, it is not eligible for organic certification. But it does meet these rigorous aquaculture farming standards:

- Hawaiian Spirulina is grown in a BioSecure zone free from pesticides, herbicides, genetically modified organisms (GMOs), and other unnatural substances.
- Hawaiian Spirulina is cultured in lined ponds. The microalgae are grown in self-contained ecosystems. This ensures no runoff from the cultured ponds into the environment, nor even the remote possibility of unwanted chemical seepage into the ponds.
- Hawaiian Spirulina regularly undergoes third-party inspections, processing inspections, and other extensive quality-control tests.
- Hawaiian Spirulina uses the same nitrogen source that wild-growing spirulina has used for billions of years.
- Cyanotech was the first company to receive the Non-GMO Project Verified seal on its spirulina from the Non-GMO Project non-profit organization.

If purity, freshness, and safety are the goals of farmers and consumers alike, then when it comes to spirulina, organic is not always best.

Chapter

6

Top Considerations When Choosing a Spirulina Brand

Know the Source

The quality of water used to grow spirulina has a major influence on the quality of the spirulina produced. Cyanotech is the only producer of spirulina that uses certified potable (drinking) water. Other spirulina producers use non-potable river or irrigation water that might contain contaminates that spirulina can absorb. And as previously stated, Cyanotech's spirulina production is in a biosecure zone and uses Ocean Chill drying to protect sensitive nutrients in spirulina.

Smell and Taste

The freshest sources of spirulina have a mild sea vegetable aroma and flavor. This is perhaps the easiest way to identify the quality of the spirulina. If the spirulina smells like rancid oil or tastes fishy, there's a good chance the producers used an organic source of nitrogen to feed their crops. Recall that organic nitrogen comes from either animal manure or decomposing plant life, both highly susceptible to bacterial infestation. Hawaiian Spirulina's clean, fresh smell and taste result from both its inorganic fertilizer mined right from the earth as well as its state-of-the-art production methods.

Nutrients and Cost

While people take spirulina to increase their energy and improve their health, not just any spirulina will accomplish these goals. When it says Hawaiian Spirulina on a product label, buyers know that no shortcut has been taken in the growing, harvesting and processing of the spirulina—all nutrients have been preserved from pond to package.

Excipients

Spirulina is a very fine powder and thus very difficult to tablet. It requires what are known as excipients, inert ingredients that make the raw material easier to make tablets. The amount and type of excipients used in tableting are crucial for quality control. Hawaiian

Spirulina contains only 1.5 percent of the highest-quality excipients. The other 98.5 percent is pure Hawaiian Spirulina. The amount and quality of the excipients can reduce not only the nutritional quality of the spirulina, but also the tablet's bioavailability in the body.

Regulation and Verification

Hawaiian Spirulina is regulated by the U.S. Food and Drug Administration (FDA) under the Dietary Supplement Health and Education Act, the State of Hawaii Department of Health, the U.S. Department of Agriculture, and the Federal Trade Commission. In addition, the company is subjected to frequent independent audits and rigorous Quality Assurance and Supplier Approval programs. The inspections consist of an intensive audit of processes and practices, including manufacturing, packaging, and labeling of Hawaiian Spirulina products according to Current Good Manufacturing Practices. The FDA has awarded Hawaiian Spirulina the GRAS (Generally Recognized as Safe) certification for its ingredients and Hawaiian Spirulina has been given the Non-GMO Project Verification seal, validating that the product contains no genetically modified organisms. Hawaiian Spirulina is also Kosher, certified gluten-free, and 100 percent vegan.

Heavy Metal Levels

In some locations, high pollution levels in the air or runoff by nearby factories contains high amounts of heavy metals. Just as spirulina absorbs harmful metals from the body, it also does the same from its environment. Grown on the Big Island's sparsely populated Kona coast, and inside Hawaii's BioSecure zone, Hawaiian Spirulina is in no danger of toxic heavy metal contamination.

Chapter

7

Recipes

A note from the Author: I like to eat spirulina, but while I'm a scientist who is very good at growing microalgae, I'm not very skilled in a kitchen. Fortunately, I have many people around me who do a good job of incorporating spirulina into food. I've turned this section of the book over to them to share some delicious spirulina recipes.

Incorporating spirulina into one's diet is the first step toward a healthier lifestyle. Adding high quality spirulina powder can turn a basic fruit smoothie into a superfood smoothie, with all the associated health benefits. It can turn a snack food like popcorn into an antioxidant mouthful. A dash of Hawaiian Spirulina adds sustained energy and wellness to every bite.

This mix of recipes filled with superfood goodness will become a favorite way to prepare foods.

- **Smoothies/Drinks:** Adding spirulina to smoothies is one of the easiest ways to incorporate spirulina daily. Just add a teaspoon to any smoothie recipe. Spirulina can also be added to other beverages.
- **Snacks:** These snack recipes are potent nutrient powerhouses. They combine whole food ingredients to create tasty, filling and satisfying snacks that can be consumed any time of day.
- **Sides:** These savory and sweet dishes pack a real superfood punch that work well on their own or with an entrée.
- **Treats:** An occasional treat fits with any healthy eating plan and when they're made with superfoods, it's a win-win.

SPIRULINA FRUIT SMOOTHIE

This refreshing smoothie uses fresh fruit and spirulina to create a tasty, nutritious, and filling drink.

MAKES 2 SERVINGS

1/2 cup yogurt

1 cup of fruit juice

1 or more of the
    following: papaya,
    peach or mango

1/2 cup of boysenberries

1 teaspoon Hawaiian
    Spirulina powder

Blend all ingredients together until smooth.

DRIED PLUM & APPLE GREEN SMOOTHIE

This is a power-packed smoothie that's ideal to drink after workouts or first thing in the morning.

MAKES 1-2 SERVINGS

1 cup vanilla yogurt
(dairy or nondairy)

8 dried plums, pitted
(prunes)

4 leaves of romaine
lettuce

1 kiwi, peeled

1/2 banana (fresh or
frozen)

1-2 tablespoons of frozen
apple-juice
concentrate

1 teaspoon Hawaiian
Spirulina powder

1/4 lemon, peeled (leave
pithy part on)

1/8 teaspoon
ground cinnamon

3 fresh mint leaves

5-6 ice cubes

Blend all ingredients together until smooth.

LEMON COCONUT SMOOTHIE

Created by superfood chef, Julie Morris.

There are many borderline magical flavor combinations in the world, with lemon and coconut easily earning their spot on that best-of list. This creamy blend tastes almost like a cheesecake, and thanks to its balance of quality protein, greens, minerals, and healthy fats, this smoothie makes an energizing meal replacement.

MAKES 16 OUNCES / 1 SERVING

1 frozen banana

1 tablespoon hemp seeds

2 tablespoons dried shredded coconut (unsweetened)

1 Medjool date, pitted

1 tablespoon your favorite vanilla protein powder

1 teaspoon Hawaiian Spirulina powder

1 tablespoon fresh lemon juice

2 tablespoons freshly grated lemon zest

1 tablespoon vanilla extract

3/4 cup almond milk

1 cup coconut water ice,* or regular ice

In a blender, combine all the ingredients except the ice, and blend until smooth and creamy. Add the ice and blend until frosty. Enjoy immediately. Makes 16 ounces (1 serving).

* Freeze coconut water in ice cube trays for enhanced smoothie flavor and extra electrolytes.

ICED SPIRULINA PEPPERMINT TEA

This refreshing tea is refreshing on a hot day and provides a nice energy boost.

MAKES APPROXIMATELY ½ GALLON OF TEA

8 bags of peppermint tea

1/2 teaspoon Hawaiian Spirulina powder

8 ounces of warm water

64 ounces of boiling water

Fresh organic mint leaves for garnish

Place the ½ teaspoon of Hawaiian Spirulina into a cup and add eight ounces of warm water. Mix together. In a separate pitcher, add 64 ounces of boiling water to eight peppermint tea bags. Steep for five minutes. Allow to cool, add spirulina mixture, and chill with ice. Garnish with mint leaves.

AVOCADO BLUEBERRY SPIRULINA TOAST

Toast doesn't have to be boring. This toast combines the healthy fat from avocado with antioxidant powerhouse blueberries and spirulina to make a filling and nutritious snack.

MAKES 2 SERVINGS

4 slices of whole grain bread

I small to medium ripe avocado

1/2 teaspoon Hawaiian Spirulina powder

1/4 cup crumbled goat cheese

1/2 cup organic blueberries, washed

Toast bread in toaster or oven. While bread is toasting, mash avocado and mix in the Hawaiian Spirulina powder. Divide the avocado mash between the four pieces of toast and spread. Sprinkle with blueberries and goat cheese.

SPIRULINA POPCORN

This common snack gets supercharged with the addition of Hawaiian Spirulina and seasonings.

MAKES 1-2 SERVINGS

Grated parmesan cheese

Garlic powder to taste

Cayenne pepper, chili pepper or paprika to taste

1 large bowl of popped corn

1 tablespoon of Hawaiian Spirulina powder

Make popcorn as usual. Mix together the seasoning ingredients. While popcorn is still warm, add seasoning mixture and shake vigorously so that the popcorn is evenly coated.

COCONUT WALNUT SPIRULINA ENERGY BITES

These bites are small packages of pure energy. Walnuts provide substance and the dates serve as a natural sweetener.

MAKES 24 BITES

20 Medjool dates, pitted

2 cups walnut pieces

1 teaspoon Hawaiian Spirulina powder

1/2 cup hemp seeds

1/4 cup unsweetened coconut flakes plus 1/4 cup for coating

Place walnuts, dates, hempseeds, Hawaiian Spirulina, and 1/4 cup of coconut into food processor and mix until it becomes sticky and starts to form a ball (around two minutes). Take dough from food processor and form one inch balls. Roll the balls into the remaining coconut to coat them. Serve immediately or refrigerate in an airtight container for up to five days.

SPIRULINA GUACAMOLE

When spirulina is added to guacamole, it gives it a rich color and skyrockets the nutritional value.

MAKES APPROXIMATELY 2 CUPS

2 large avocados

Cayenne pepper

2 medium tomatoes

1 tablespoon finely
chopped onion

1/2 tablespoon minced
garlic

2 teaspoons Hawaiian
Spirulina powder

Fresh lime juice to taste

2 tablespoons salsa

Salt to taste

Mash avocados. Add all other ingredients and blend well. Chill in the refrigerator for 20 minutes before serving with veggies or chips.

HAWAIIAN SPIRULINA TRAIL MIX BARS

These raw bars make great energy-boosting snacks.

MAKES APPROXIMATELY 12 BARS

1/2 cup raw almonds

1/4 cup coconut

1 cup chopped dates

1/4 cup shredded coconut

1/4 cup pepitas

1/2 cup dried fruit,
   roughly chopped

1/4 cup sunflower seeds

1 teaspoon Hawaiian
   Spirulina powder

Place all ingredients in a food processor and pulse for 30 seconds. Roll all ingredients into a ball and spread into an 8x8 pan lined with wax or parchment paper. Allow to set for 10-15 minutes, and cut into 12 bars. Keep in airtight container for up to a week.

VEG OUT STUFFED PEPPERS

These peppers make a great side or entrée.

MAKES 2 SERVINGS

2 fresh bell peppers, any color (bottoms and tops sliced off)

1 cup cooked quinoa

2 teaspoons extra virgin olive oil

1 onion, finely chopped

6 oz. mushrooms, chopped small

1/2 cup diced red peppers

1/2 cup diced cherry tomatoes

fresh ground black pepper to taste

1 cup crumbled goat cheese

1 teaspoon Hawaiian Spirulina powder

Preheat oven to 375. Sauté onions, mushrooms and peppers until softened, and sprinkle with ground black pepper. Add mixture to quinoa and mix in diced tomatoes and Hawaiian Spirulina. Place the pepper "shells" in a small baking dish and fill with the quinoa and veggie mixture. Wrap in foil and bake for 30 minutes. After 30 minutes, remove from oven and sprinkle with goat cheese. Bake an additional 15 to 20 minutes until the goat cheese starts to melt and brown.

TOFU SALAD

This protein and nutrient rich salad is a great lunch option.

MAKES 1-2 SERVINGS

8 ounces firm tofu

1 bell pepper (green or red)

2 medium tomatoes

1 medium zucchini

1 medium grated carrot

2 stalks celery

2 spring onions, finely chopped

1 tablespoon tamari or soy sauce

Generous pinch of basil, thyme, and marjoram

Hot pepper sauce or cayenne pepper (to taste)

1 teaspoon Hawaiian Spirulina powder

Mix all ingredients together. Almost any combination of raw vegetables can be put into a tofu salad.

THAT'S A SUPER WRAP

This wrap is carb free and loaded with nutrients from the veggies and spirulina.

MAKES ONE WRAP

1 collard green leaf,
   main stem removed

1 teaspoon hummus

1/2 teaspoon Hawaiian
   Spirulina powder

1/4 cup shredded carrots

1/4 cup thinly sliced
   avocado

Lay collard green leaf flat on a plate. Spread with hummus and layer other ingredients. Sprinkle Hawaiian Spirulina on top and roll up to eat. Mix in any of your favorite raw veggies for more variety.

SUPERFOOD GRAINS

This grains recipe is sweetened with natural fruit and peppers and Hawaiian Spirulina boosts its nutrient power.

MAKES 4 SERVINGS

I cup of your favorite grains blend, cooked (e.g. barley, wild rice and quinoa)

I large bell pepper diced (or your favorite raw veggie)

1/2 cup raisins

I teaspoon Hawaiian Spirulina powder

Your favorite spices to taste

Mix all ingredients together and serve warm or chilled.

SPIRULINA AVOCADO CUCUMBER BITES

These bites are wonderful to serve at a party or to make and serve as an appetizer before a meal.

MAKES 6 TO 8 BITES

1 large organic cucumber

1 ripe avocado

Pinch of Kosher salt

1/2 ripe organic roma tomato, diced

1 teaspoon fresh lime juice

1/2 teaspoon Hawaiian Spirulina powder

organic grape tomatoes for garnish

Cut cucumber into thick one inch slices (you should be able to get six to eight chunks from a large cucumber). Scoop flesh out from center of cucumber. Cut avocado in half and scoop out flesh. Mash with a fork and mix with all remaining ingredients except for the grape tomatoes. Scoop into each cucumber bite and garnish with half a grape tomato. Serve immediately.

SPIRULINA PESTO (pasta sauce)

Increase the nutritional value of this traditional basil pesto by adding Hawaiian Spirulina.

MAKES 4 SERVINGS

1 packed cup fresh basil leaves

3-5 tablespoons extra virgin olive oil

2 tablespoons parmesan cheese

3 cloves garlic

2 teaspoons Hawaiian Spirulina powder

pinch of salt

2 ounces pine nuts, macadamia nuts, almonds, or walnuts

Blend all ingredients and toss with your favorite warm pasta or pasta salads.

SPINACH, KALE, AND SPIRULINA BITES

With the easy preparation and ultra-nutritious ingredients in this healthy snack or side dish recipe, these Spinach, Kale and Spirulina Bites will become an instant family favorite.

MAKES 12-15 BITES

1-2 cups frozen spinach

1 bunch of kale, chopped into small pieces

2 cups cooked quinoa

1/2 cup cheese

1 onion diced

3 eggs beaten

spices to taste

1 teaspoon Hawaiian Spirulina powder

Preheat oven to 425 degrees. Sauté onions, spinach and kale until onions are translucent and spinach and kale are wilted. Mix green veggie mixture with all other ingredients. Roll into balls and place on cookie sheet lined with parchment paper or sprayed with cooking spray. Bake in oven for 30 minutes. Serve over greens or brown rice noodles or eat as appetizers.

SUPERFOOD CHOCOLATE HEARTS

Recipe created by superfood chef, Julie Morris

No chocolate molds? No problem. Just pour the chocolate on a chilled porcelain plate, refrigerate until hard, and snap apart in large chunks with a dull knife for an elegant chocolate bark.

MAKES 24 SMALL HEARTS

1/2 cup melted cacao butter*

1/4 cup cacao powder

2 teaspoons Hawaiian Spirulina powder

1/8 teaspoon vanilla powder

pinch sea salt

2 tablespoons agave nectar

1/4 cup mixed finely minced toppings (such as goji berries, dried dragonfruit, and culinary gold foil)

Place the cacao butter in a medium bowl. Use a wire whisk to mix in the cacao powder, spirulina, vanilla powder and sea salt – whisk until completely smooth. Add the agave, and whisk vigorously to combine. A teaspoon at a time, carefully pour into chocolate molds – such as small hearts, or desired shapes. Sprinkle the tops lightly with minced toppings of choice. Place in the freezer for 10 minutes, or until chocolate is completely solidified. Snap hardened chocolate out of the molds and serve. Chocolate may be stored in the refrigerator or at room temperature, but will soften in very warm environments.

* Melt cacao butter shavings over very low heat until liquefied. Be careful not to burn – err on the side of lower heat.

SUPERBERRY CRISPY RICE TREATS

Recipe created by superfood chef, Julie Morris

Filled with satisfying crispy-crunch and big berry flavor, these irresistible treats are an ideal back-to-school reward, or just a fun not-so-naughty sweet snack.

MAKES 16 2-INCH SQUARES

1/4 cup + 2 tablespoons sliced almonds, divided

1 cup + 2 tablespoons freeze-dried blueberries, divided

3 cups crispy brown rice cereal (use lowest sugar brand available)

1 1/2 teaspoons Hawaiian Spirulina powder

3 tablespoons acai powder

1/2 cup almond butter

1/2 cup maple syrup

1 teaspoon vanilla extract

2 tablespoons chia seeds

Line an 8×8 baking pan with parchment paper, hanging excess paper over the sides of the pan as flaps, for easy removal. Set aside.

In a food processor or spice grinder, combine 1/4 cup of the almonds, and 2 tablespoons of the freeze dried blueberries. Process into a coarse purple powder. Set aside.

In a medium bowl, mix together the crispy rice, spirulina and acai. In a separate large bowl, whisk together the almond butter, maple syrup, and vanilla until smooth. Add the rice mixture and mix until evenly coated. Fold in chia seeds, and 1 cup of freeze-dried blueberries. Toss to coat thoroughly. Transfer the mixture into the prepared pan in an even layer, and smooth out to cover the surface of the pan. Sprinkle the prepared almond-blueberry powder over the whole exposed layer, then scatter the remaining 2 tablespoons sliced almonds on top. Use a the back of a spatula to press the treats firmly until flat and compact. Refrigerate for 1 hour before cutting into 2-inch squares.

Crispy rice treats may be stored refrigerated or kept at room temperature, and will last for up to one week.

Chapter

8

Frequently Asked Questions

Q: What is Spirulina?
A: Spirulina is microscopic blue-green microalgae that grow naturally in fresh water ponds and lakes in warm, sunny environments. Spirulina has been used as a food source for centuries. It is considered the most complete naturally cultivated nutrient in the world, and Hawaiian Spirulina has approximately double the levels of key nutrients compared to other brands. Hawaiian Spirulina provides:

- Approximately 60 percent complete digestible protein - it contains every essential amino acid;
- Contains more carotenoids than any other whole food and is an excellent source of vitamins A, K, B12 and iron, manganese and chromium;
- Best wholefood source of gamma linoleic acid (GLA) – an essential fatty acid, necessary for human health. It plays a crucial role in brain function as well as normal growth and development;
- Rich in vitamins, minerals, trace elements, chlorophyll and enzymes.

Q: What are the benefits of using Spirulina?
A: Spirulina strenghtens the immune system and boosts energy levels. In addition to being a wonderful source of protein, spirulina contains more carotenoids than any other whole food. It is also rich in antioxidants and phytonutrients. There is overwhelming clinical evidence to show that Hawaiian Spirulina also supports cardiovascular, eye, brain and skin health.

Q: Who should take Hawaiian Spirulina?
A: Everyone! Hawaiian Spirulina is an ideal food supplement for people of all ages and lifestyles.

Q: What are some of the key nutrients in Hawaiian Spirulina?
A: It is a complete protein with high levels of antioxidants, vitamins and phytochemicals

including:

- Beta Carotene: Necessary for healthy skin, good vision, and a healthy immune system.
- Vitamin B12: An essential vitamin required for proper red blood cell formation, neurological function, and DNA synthesis.
- Vitamin K1 & Vitamin K2: Essential vitamins known to promote blood clotting and support bone health. Recent studies have confirmed that vitamin K2 may help osteoporosis and cardiovascular diseases.
- Superoxide Dismutase (SOD): An enzyme that acts as both an antioxidant and anti-inflammatory in the body, neutralizing free radicals and helping to repair cells, for age related degeneration.
- Zeaxanthin: A carotenoid and powerful antioxidant that fights free radical damage with specific benefits for eye and cellular health.
- Phycocyanin: The blue pigment color in nature, only found in spirulina. Supports kidney, liver and brain health.
- Iron: Essential in the formation of red blood cells and transportation of oxygen throughout the body. Iron assists the memory and helps build resistance to infection, stress and disease.

Q: How much Hawaiian Spirulina should I take each day?

A: The suggested serving for Hawaiian Spirulina is three grams a day. Hawaiian Spirulina is available in tablet and powder form:

Tablet bottles
- 500 mg - six tablets a day
- 1,000 mg - three tablets a day

Powder bottles
- One teaspoon mixed with liquid

Q: Should I be concerned about the high amount of vitamin A in Hawaiian Spirulina?

A: No, the vitamin A activity of Hawaiian Spirulina comes from natural beta carotene. Beta carotene is a precursor to vitamin A--the human body converts beta carotene into vitamin A on an as-needed basis. There is no toxicity level for beta carotene, so there is no need to worry about taking too much.

Q: Are spirulina tablets absorbed by the body as well as powder?

A: In terms of absorption, the tablets take longer to breakdown once ingested, but this can actually be a good thing. There are many enzymes in Hawaiian Spirulina (for example super oxide dismutase is an outstanding antioxidant the human body actually produces itself as a defense mechanism against harmful reactive oxygen species). Enzymes are often destroyed by stomach acids during digestion, however spirulina tablets are only partially digested in the stomach. Their digestion is completed in the intestines. In the intestines there are no stomach acids present, so you can get the full benefit of these vital enzymes.

Q: How should Spirulina be stored?

A: The single most important thing you can do to preserve spirulina once it has been opened is to refrigerate it. If kept cold (or even frozen) there should be a negligible loss of nutrients.

Q: Can children take Hawaiian Spirulina?

A: Yes. Hawaiian Spirulina is just a food and can be given to children. In fact, it's beneficial for children who don't like to eat vegetables. The powder can be easily mixed in a smoothie or a shake.

Q: Can pregnant women take Hawaiian Spirulina?

A: Yes. The key things in spirulina for pregnant and nursing mothers are iron, protein and the bioavailability of all the nutrition. Pregnant women should consult their health care professional.

Q: Since Hawaiian Spirulina contains iron and is a source of vitamin K1 & K2, is it safe for anyone to take, regardless of their age?

A: Spirulina is safe for all ages, however, people taking prescription or over-the-counter medication should consult their health care professional.

About the Author

Dr. Gerald Cysewski is recognized as a world authority on microalgae. He has over 35 years of experience in microalgae research and commercial production of microalgae products. His work on microalgae in 1976 was supported by the National Science Foundation at the University of California at Santa Barbara where he was an assistant professor in the department of chemical and nuclear engineering. He carried on his work at Battelle Northwest as group leader of microalgae research.

Dr. Cysewski founded Cyanotech Corporation in 1983 in Washington State, and has served in executive and scientific positions at Cyanotech. After several years as president and chief executive officer, Dr. Cysewski returned to his true love of science when he became Cyanotech's chief scientific officer in 2008. Dr. Cysewski holds a bachelor of science in chemical engineering from the University of Washington and a doctorate in chemical engineering from the University of California, Berkeley.

Endnotes

1 "How Many Fruits and Vegetables Do You Need?" Centers for Disease Control and Prevention website. As of April 3, 2015: http://www.fruitsandveggiesmorematters.org/wp-content/uploads/UserFiles/File/pdf/resources/cdc/howMany_Brochure.pdf

2 Ronald H. Henson (Nov.-Dec. 1990). "Spirulina Algae Improves Japanese Fish Feeds," *Aquaculture Magazine*, pp. 38-43.

3 Larry Switzer (1982). *Spirulina: The Whole Food Revolution*, New York: Bantam Books.

4 "Spirulina's Nutritional Analysis," Natural Ways website. As of March 15, 2015: http://www.naturalways.com/spirulina-analysis.htm

5 "Supplements," University of Maryland Medical Center website. As of March 15, 2015: http://umm.edu/health/medical/altmed/supplement/omega6-fatty-acids

6 Praneel Datla (July 2011). *The Wonder Molecule Called Phycocyanin*, India: Parry Nutraceuticals.

7 USDA National Nutrient Database for Standard Reference, United States Department of Agriculture website. As of September 2015: http://ndb.nal.usda.gov/

8 "Zeaxanthin Facts." As of February 26, 2015: http://www.ezeyes.info/ezeyes_Zeaxanthin.aspx

9 "Zeaxanthin Facts." As of February 26, 2015: http://www.ezeyes.info/ezeyes_Zeaxanthin.aspx

10 N. Shimidzu, M. Goto, and W. Miki (1996). "Carotenoids as singlet oxygen quenchers in marine organisms," *Fisheries Science*, Vol. 62, No. 1, pp. 134-137.

11 "Hemoglobin and Functions of Iron," UCSF Medical Center website. As of February 26, 2015: http://www.ucsfhealth.org/education/hemoglobin_and_functions_of_iron/

12 "Vitamin K2: The Missing Nutrient." As of February 26, 2015: http://chriskresser.com/vitamin-k2-the-missing-nutrient

13 "Vitamin K1 or K2 Effective for Bone Boosting Potential: Study." As of February 26, 2015: http://www.nutraingredients-usa.com/Research/Vitamin-K1-or-K2-effective-for-bone-boosting-potential-Study.

14 E.M. Keithley, C. Canto, Q.Y. Zheng, X. Wang, N. Fischel-Ghodsian, and K.R. Johnson (July 28, 2005). "Cu/Zn superoxide dismutase and age-related hearing loss," *Hearing Research*, Vol. 209, No. 1-2, pp. 76-85.

15 V.L. Kinnula (August 2005). "Focus on antioxidant enzymes and antioxidant strategies in smoking related airway diseases," *Thorax*, Vol. 60, No. 8, pp. 693-700.

16 E. Nozik-Grayck, H.B. Suliman, and C.A. Piantadosi (December 2005). "Extracellular superoxide dismutase," *International Journal of Biochemistry & Cell Biology*, Vol. 37, No. 12, pp. 2466-71.

17 H.J. Park, Y.J. Lee, H.K. Ryu, M.H. Kim, H.W. Chung, and W.Y. Kim (August 2008). "A randomized double-blind, placebo-controlled study to establish the effects of spirulina in elderly Koreans," *Annals of Nutrition Metabolism*, Vol. 52, No. 4, pp. 322-328.

18 H. K. Lu, C.C., Hsieh, J.J., Hsu, Y.K., Yang, and H.N. Chou (September 2006). "Preventive effects of Spirulina platensis on skeletal muscle damage under exercise-induced oxidative stress," *European Journal of Applied Physiology*, Vol. 98, No. 2, pp. 220-226.

19 M. Kalafati, A.Z. Jamuartas, M.G. Nikolaidis, V. Paschalis, A.A. Theodorou, G.K. Sakellariou, Y. Koutedakis, and D. Kouretas (January 2010). "Ergogenic and antioxidant effects of spirulina supplementation in humans," *Medicine & Science in Sports & Exercise*, Vol. 42, No. 1, pp. 142-151.

20 H. K. Lu, C.C., Hsieh, J.J., Hsu, Y.K., Yang, and H.N. Chou (September 2006). "Preventive effects of Spirulina platensis on skeletal muscle damage under exercise-induced oxidative stress," *European Journal of Applied Physiology*, Vol. 98, No. 2, pp. 220-226.

21 Hawaiian Spirulina Survey (May-July 2011). SurveyMonkey, Inc., website. As of April 26, 2015: https://www.surveymonkey.com/results/SM-BYNSG9W9/

22 C. Selmi, P.S. Leung, L. Fischer, B. German, C.Y. Yang, T.P. Kenny, G.R. Cysewski, and M.E. Gershwin (May 2011). "The effects of Spirulina on anemia and immune function in senior citizens," *Cellular & Molecular Immunology*, Vol. 8, pp. 248-254.

23 A. Hernandez-Corona, I. Nieves, M. Meckes, G. Chamorro, and B.L. Barron (December 2002). "Antiviral activity of Spirulina maxima against herpes simplex virus type 2," *Antiviral Research*, Vol. 56, No. 3, pp. 379-385.

24 O.B. Gorobets, L.P. Blinkova, and A.P. Baturo (November-December 2002). "Action of spirulina platensis on bacterial viruses," *Zhurnal Mikrobiologii, Epidemiologii, i Immunobiologii*, No. 6, pp. 18-21.

25 M. Misbahuddin, A.Z. Islam, S. Khandker, Islam Ifthaker-Al-Mahmud, and N. Anjumanara (2006). "Efficacy of spirulina extract plus zinc in patients of chronic arsenic poisoning: A randomized placebo-controlled study," *Clinical Toxicology*, Vol. 44, No. 2, pp. 135-141.

26 C.D. Upasan and R. Balaraman (April 2003). "Protective effect of spirulina on lead induced deleterious changes in the lipid peroxidation and endogenous antioxidants in rats," *Phytotherapy Research*, Vol. 17, No. 4, pp. 330-334.

27 C.D. Upasan and R. Balaraman (April 2003). "Protective effect of spirulina on lead induced deleterious changes in the lipid peroxidation and endogenous antioxidants in rats," *Phytotherapy Research*, Vol. 17, No. 4, pp. 330-334.

28 N. Simsek, A. Karadeniz, Y. Kalkan, O.N. Keles, and B. Unal (May 2009). "Spirulina platensis feeding inhibited the anemia- and leucopenia-induced lead and cadmium in rats," *Journal of Hazardous Materials*, Vol. 164, No. 2-3, pp. 1304-09.

29 N. Paniagua-Castro, G. Escalona-Cardoso, D. Hernandez-Navarro, R. Perez-Pasten, and G. Chamorro-Cevallos (April 2011). "Spirulina (Arthrospira) protects against cadmium-induced teratogenic damage in mice," *Journal of Medicinal Food*, Vol. 14, No. 4, pp. 398-404.

30 S. K. Saha, M. Misbahuddin, and A.U. Ahmed (January 2010). "Comparison between the effects of alcohol and hexane extract of spirulina in arsenic removal from isolated tissues," *Mymensingh Medical Journal*, Vol. 19, No. 1, pp. 27-31.

31 L.P. Loseva and I.V. Dardynskaya (September 1993). "Spirulina-natural sorbent of radionucleides" Research Institute of Radiation Medicine, Minsk, Belarus. Paper presented at the 6th International Congress of Applied Algology, Czech Republic

32 K. Moorhead, B. Capelli, and G. Cysweski (2012). *Spirulina Nature's Superfood*, Kailua-Kona, HI: Cyanotech Corporation.

33 L.C. Wu, J.A. Ho, M.C. Shieh, and I.W. Lu (May 2005). "Antioxidant and antiproliferative activities of spirulina and chlorella water extracts," *Journal of Agricultural and Food Chemistry*, Vol. 53, No. 10, pp. 4207-12.

34 G. Puyfoulhoux, J.M. Rouanet, P. Besancon, B. Baroux, J.C. Baccou, and B. Caporiccio (March 2001). "Iron availability from iron-fortified spirulina by an in vitro digestion/Caco-2 cell culture model," *Journal of Agricultural and Food Chemistry*, Vol. 39, No. 3, pp. 1625-29.

35 M. De, A. Halder, T. Chakraborty, U. Das, S. Paul, A. De, J. Banerjee, T. Chatterjee, and S. De (May 2011). "Incidence of anemia and effect of nutritional supplementation on women in rural and tribal populations of eastern and northeastern India," *Hematology*, Vol. 16, No. 3, pp. 190-192.

36 R. Kapoor and U. Mehta (1998). "Supplementary effect of spirulina on hematological status of rats during pregnancy and lactation," *Plant Foods for Human Nutrition*, Vol. 52, No. 4, pp. 315-324.

37 Y. Wang, C.F. Chang, J. Chou, H.L. Chen, X. Deng, B.K. Harvey, J.L. Cadet, and P.C. Bickford (May 2005). "Dietary supplementation with blueberries, spinach, or spirulina reduces ischemic brain damage," *Experimental Neurology*, Vol. 193, No. 1, pp. 75-84.

38 A.D. Bachstetter, J. Jernberg, A. Schlunk, J.L. Vila, C. Hudson, M.J. Cole, R.D. Shytle, J. Tan, P.R. Sanberg, C.D. Sanberg, C. Borlongan, Y. Kaneko, N. Tajiri, C. Gemma, and P.C. Bickford (May 2010). "Spirulina promotes stem cell genesis and protects against LPS induced declines in neural stem

cell proliferation. *PLOS ONE,* Vol. 5, No. 5.

39 M. Gargouri, F. Chorbel-Koubaa, M. Bonenfant-Magne, C. Magne, X. Dauvergne, R. Ksouri, Y. Krichen, C. Abdelly, and A. El Feki (July 2012). "Spirulina or dandelion-enriched diets of mothers alleviates lead-induced damages in brain and cerebellum of newborn rats," *Food and Chemical Toxicology,* Vol. 50, No. 7, pp. 2303-10.

40 N. Patro, A. Sharmam, K. Kariaya, and I. Patro (October 2011). "Spirulina platensis protects neurons via suppression of glial activation and peripheral sensitization leading to restoration of motor function in collagen-induced arthritic rats," *Indian Journal of Experimental Biology,* Vol. 39, No. 10, pp. 739-748.

41 J.H. Hwang, I.T. Lee, K.C. Jeng, M.F. Wang, R.C. Hou, S.M. Wu, and Y.C. Chang (2011). "Spriulina prevents memory dysfunction, reduces oxidative stress damage and augments antioxidant activity in senescence-accelerated mice," *Journal of Nutritional Science and Vitaminology* (Tokyo), Vol. 57, No. 2, pp. 186-191.

42 S. Thaakur and R. Sravanthi (September 2010). "Neuroprotective effect of spirulina in cerebral ischemia-reperfusion injury in rats," *Journal of Neural Transmission,* Vol. 117, No. 9, pp. 1083-91.

43 G. Chamorro, M. Perez-Albiter, N. Serrano-Garcia, J.J. Mares-Samano, and P. Rojas, P. (October 2006). "Spirulina maxima pretreatment partially protects against 1-methyl-4-phenyl-1,2,3,6-tetrahydropyridine neurotoxicity," *Nutritional Neuroscience,* Vol. 9, No. 5-6, pp. 207-212.

44 M.F. McCarty, J. Barroso-Aranda, and F. Contreras (March 2010). "Oral phcocyanobilin may diminish the pathogenicity of activated brain microglia in neurodegenerative disorders," *Medical Hypotheses,* Vol. 74, No. 3, pp. 601-605.

45 S.H. Kim, C. Shin, S.K. Min, S.M. Jung, and H.S. Shin (Feb. 2012). "In vitro evaluation of the effects of electrospun PCL nanofiber mats containing the microalgae spirulina (Arthrospira) extract on primary astrocytes," *Colloids and Surfaces B: Biointerfaces,* Vol. 90, pp. 113-118.

46 E.P. Sabina, J. Samual, S. RajappaRamya, S. Patel, N. Mandal, P. Pranatharthiiharan, P.P. Mishra, and M.K. Rasool (2009). "Hepatoprotective and antioxidant potential of spirulina fusiformis on acetaminophen-induced hepatotoxicity in mice," *International Journal of Integrative Biology,* Vol. 6, No. 1, pp. 1-5.

47 P.V. Torres-Durán, R. Miranda-Zamora, M.C. Paredes-Carbajal, D. Mascher, J. Blé-Castillo, J.C. Díaz-Zagoya, M.A. Juárez-Oropeza. "Studies on the preventive effect of spirulina maxima on fatty liver development induced by carbon tetrachloride, in the rat," *Journal of Ethnopharmacology,* Vol. 64 (1999), pp. 141-147.

48 O. Sinanoglu, A.N. Yener, S. Ekici, A. Midi, and F.B. Aksungar (December 2012). "The protective effects of spirulina in cyclophosphamide induced nephrotoxicity and urotoxicity in rats," *Urology,* Vol. 80, No. 6, p. 1392.

49 A. Kuhad, N. Tirkey, S. Pilkhwal, K. Chopra (2006). "Renoprotective effect of Spirulina fusiformis on cisplatin-induced oxidative stress and renal dysfunction in rats," *Renal Failure*, Vol. 28, No. 3, pp. 247-254.

50 S.M. Farooq, D. Asoka, R. Sakthivel, P. Kalaiselvi, and P. Varalakshmi (October 2004). "Salubrious effect of C-phycocyanin against oxalate-mediated renal cell injury," *Clinica Chimica Acta*, Vol. 348, No. 1-2, pp. 199-205.

51 M.K. Sharma, A. Sharma, A. Kumar, and M. Kumar (June 2007). "Evaluation of protective efficacy of Spirulina fusiformis against mercury induced nephrotoxicity in Swiss albino mice," *Food and Chemical Toxicology*, Vol. 45, No. 6, pp. 879-887.

52 A. Karaeniz, A. Yildirim, N. Simsek, Y. Kalkan, and F. Celebi (November 2008). "Spirulina platensis protects against gentamicin-induced nephrotoxicy in rats," *Phytotherapy Research*, Vol. 22, No. 11, pp. 1506-10.

53 M.E. Gershwin and Amha Belay, eds. (2008). *Spirulina in Human Nutrition and Health*, Boca Raton, FL: CRC Press.

54 P.V. Torres-Duran, A. Ferreira-Hermosillo, and M.A. Juarez-Oropeza (November 2007). "Antihyperlipidemic and antihypertensive effects of Spirulina maxima in an open sample of Mexican population: A preliminary report," *Lipids in Health and Disease*, Vol. 6, No. 33.

55 H.J. Park, Y.J. Lee, H.K. Ryu, M.H. Kim, H.W. Chung, and W.Y. Kim (August 2008). "A randomized double-blind, placebo-controlled study to establish the effects of spirulina in elderly Koreans," *Annals of Nutrition and Metabolism*, Vol. 54, No. 4, pp. 322-328.

56 B. Capelli and G. Cysewski, G. (2010). "Potential health benefits of spirulina microalgae: A review of the existing literature," *Nutrafoods*, Vol. 9, No. 2, pp. 19-26.